CANDLESHOE

CANDLESHOE

Rennie Parker

To Lorna
Best wishes !
from
Rennie

Market Deeping 19/3/22

Shoestring Press

Printed by imprintdigital
Upton Pyne, Exeter
www.imprintdigital.net

Typeset by types of light
typesoflight@gmail.com

Published by Shoestring Press
19 Devonshire Avenue, Beeston, Nottingham, NG9 1BS
(0115) 925 1827
www.shoestringpress.co.uk

First published 2014
Copyright © Rennie Parker

Cover image by the author, copyright © 2014

The moral right of the author has been asserted

ISBN 978 1 907356 94 0

ACKNOWLEDGEMENTS

Some of the poems appeared in *Borderville* (Shoestring, 2011) and others were previously in *Newborough County* (Shoestring, 2001).

Thanks are due to the following magazines, organisations, and anthologies, where most of the poems were published individually: *The Rialto, Seam, Leviathan, Other Poetry, Reactions 3* (Pen & Inc, 2002) *Reactions 4* (Pen & Inc, 2003) Ragged Raven Press anthology 2005, *Buzz* (Templar Poetry, 2008), *Mirehouse/Ways with Words* 2009, *Critical Survey, The Interpreter's House, Iron Book of New Humorous Verse* (Iron Press, 2010), *Under the Radar, Get Me Out Of Here* (Grey Hen, 2011).

Gill Hands' poem 'Devil's Advocate' (Iron, *Humorous Verse*) influenced 'took my sign to the crossroads', and thanks to Chris Kemp for suggesting its title.

CONTENTS

PROLOGUE

If you should see me walking
look away – it wasn't me you saw
for I walk faster than the wind,
it was a remaining shadow on the wall.
If you should hear me speak, do not reply –
the moment lives elsewhere, another time
imagine another voice you might have heard
for I have gone. It is the song
alone you hear, the crowded air.

FIRST AND SECOND ENTRANCE

I.

Green lanes shear off at the bend
their *quattrocento* pines clash

with sturdy local briars,
stiff-backed hairbrushes rock,
thorn springing the spray.

                I had bounced
down the wrong rutted track
Gorse Hill Lane New England Farm
to a tin-roof locked chapel,
its flèche straight from the inventory
of Villard d'Honnecourt,
its gate laced with warnings of Rural Theft.

The wind blows overtones –
dust and a loose branch prancing across the footway,
art being a church with no walls.

II.

This time it's a different same grey horse
the distant baying of bloodhounds
come for the last Prior

and I have walked here in medieval fashion
the scratching of holly on the threshhold
like someone else waiting outside.

The wind changes patterns on the light-crushed floor,
a cast iron chair before me
is the Grand Inquisitor
in all his twisted metal.

How many pilgrims here?
Many, friend
with their customary graffiti
trapped flies in the leaded pane.
Leave no mark, no sign

leave your shield at the gate
everything you own.

IMPOSITION AND BIRDLIGHT

Nest building on the way, two people
hand in hand are wandering the inland dunes.

At the counterweighted gate a brand
new butter-brown statue in smooth finished wood
carrying a book and larded with fresh bird-doo,
two peeled turves at his sandalled feet.

With sharp-cut features and taller than me
but with hands the same size, he has come out here
to be cemented in like all his kind
even though it looks as if he is walking away,
the keys of the kingdom up his stiff triangular sleeve.

And the bird-scarers are going *bang* and *blast*
their armadas retorting somewhere beyond
that white-bag installation like a spread-out word
which don't fool the canniest birds.

                              The farmer too,
lining his fault-free pristine electric fence
near a thornbush intricate as embroidery,
moles have spread everywhere in so short a time
little rotavators turning the crops –
the whole point of being here to see how the land will lie.

Our first two people have gone, but another two
hand in hand come tramping the gravel approach
see the new statue, smile
rub him on the shoulder: *a fine place to be, Brother Wood,*
                              you'll like it here.

WILD-HAIRED AND DUMPY, WITH COLOURS THAT CLASHED, HER DAUGHTER, EIGHTEEN, LOOKED TWELVE

....but there's no work, there's no work!
Cheryl earns more than my husband, she's booked up
That's why we're here. She's turned professional now,
Weddings, corporate dinners, that sort of thing.

We'd do anything to move, the damp is so bad.
The house – oh that was *another* complete mistake.

It's incomers, incomers, they don't like noise
No church bells, no tractors, no cocks,
....three stiff letters from the Council
And now the bloody landlord is throwing us out.
'You'll have to go!'

Haven't you noticed
When people come here they spread themselves about
As if they owned the place? Well we're not like that no.
I'm not an incomer, I *married* a man from round here....
They'll never be accepted.

The house is so small
You have to go outside if you want to turn round.
There's hardly any house to throw us out of.
Cheryl now,
Cheryl must do her practice every day. Mustn't you, love?

You don't mind do you I'll move my stuff off here
You see we haven't got a television,
Whenever we find one we tend to go berserk
Specially when it's University Challenge.

Farming is at rock bottom. It *can't* get worse.
Pensioners and rich retirees
Are all you find round here –

Every time the pig-man goes to his field
They jump up and down. It's the smell
Or too much mud
Or too many animals making the wrong kind of shit.

We tried keeping chickens: it didn't work
The man who rented the land
Asked for it back. You know what he did?
Ornamental trees, those stubby ones,
He covered his seven acres in useless trees.
And what does it *do?*

I know the incomers' gardens. Marigolds
Machine-punched into the floor at three inch intervals.
Depressing.
Take my word they're like that TV ad
Wishing they lived in the good old days
Their very own Merchant-Ivory estate
Except it's bastard England.

WOULD YOU LIKE SOME BISCUITS WITH THAT TEA?

I know I can talk to you, you look like a Pisces. Well,
You wouldn't believe how big this house can feel.
Here's some magazines. Is the room OK?

I think I'll have to sell this place next year.
My ex, he won't pay up. It's all my fault.
My friends have tried to drill it into me:

'He's done it once, he'll surely do it again'.
And now he's off with a young piece down in Kent.
He left me with the lot, the house

The bills, the kids, the debts he wouldn't pay.
Of course she's half his age and full of sex.
Would you like some biscuits with that tea?

I didn't think he was the type, you know.
We'd moved round fourteen towns in twenty years
Just for his career. It drove me nuts

Decorating all those endless rooms,
More horrid squares for living in. And yes –
He said I was the homely, clinging one.

'You're so materialistic', he would spit
But when he brought his ghastly friends back here
I lived through hell if everything wasn't right.

And now he's gone. You're looking quite dismayed.
On second thoughts, he sounds just like the type
Doesn't he. I never saw it coming.

BUTTERWICK LOW

Alas, *girasole*
it is the wrong time of year for you.
Your torches are extinguished
in a line from Marjoram's Motors to Deeping St. Nicholas.
There is a place called Malice Farm,
there's another place called Tongue End
and the birds are pecking your eyes out
in the blackened stumps of January.

Meanwhile the turbines are lording it,
they cartwheel across the fen
slicing the wind to size –
and you are more forlorn than ever,
the chewed bristles of an old brush.

I am wishing you slow summers
under the pressing heat.
I am hoping to see your gargantuan heads
follow my car as it glints past
on the stagecoach route to Spalding.
But now you are the bent skewers after the barbecue,
what's left of the trashed cabinet.

Alas, *girasole*
the tractor is coming for you
and the road-salt gritter is worrying on
with hot stones rattling at its heels.

IN FEAR OF REGIONAL WOOLSHOPS

wonder what it is about the woolshops
that and the yellow window film they use
and the lopsided non-humanly-
coloured mannequins with askew
synthetic wigs. Oh help..... sheer terror.....
how I'd cross the street to avoid
and the way those creatures lean,
fingers splayed. Who buys the goods
in there? Who wants a pattern for
that gear? Who lives to wear
a striped beret in tan and faded aqua,
whose needles clack and tick?
And then it's how the viscid sickness clings
to throw its gloomy cast on lines
of hooks and eyes, and flabby haber-
dashery from twenty years behind;
there's one in every town like this
down bricky backstreets, offset ex-resorts
where people still have furs in closets,
pantries, lard, and collar-studs; is one
of these near you, its flies,
a mildewed grosgrain roller blind,
a till stuck on 'No Sale', its keys
like those on a vintage Remington
and worse, oh worst of all, the sight
of a chalk-white creased assistant
reaching across the stale expanse
whose features look stitched on.

EVIDENCE AT THE DIGGING SITE

Nobody there except Fool
The larks playing their clockwork
Above precisely shadowed turf
In the smallness of early April
With an unseemly temperature
Warming the distant brick watertower.
OK Fool I have given in
You can lead me wherever you want
Small animals have been here,
Their excavation marks out every site
They don't know why they never let it alone.

Fool, your place is cut off at the knees
Stumps barely covered
Prey to the ant and the shrike
With hundreds of years at their disposal.
Don't worry they'll find the evidence
And look who's been here already
Her footsteps blunting the soil.

THE DIFFICULT SURFACE OF LINCOLNSHIRE

In comes Fool, lover of naming and layers.
Here she has planted her feet, here and here.
'The Distribution of Silver Street Kiln-Type Pottery'
Is one such prominent title.

The uncertainty of borders fought over
Are blurred under her feet,
Eyebright and bog myrtle threading the wastelands
Are Fool in the vacancy of creation.

She has got the variable districts sorted:
Winnibriggs, Aveland and Threo
Their medieval manors like outposts
On stained, flooded ground

And strangers with their obtuse new inventions
Dividing sea from land. The work never ends
On tidal reaches where the best names are
Vinegar Middle and Roaring Middle

Blinking their lightship messages –
O Fool, careful in shallows flipping the cockleshells
Fool soaked with the sea's ink, wading
With back to the shelving mud-banks,

There's more names in an acre of soil
Than the whole of the district library
Whose white vans travel slowly, slowly
Up Labour In Vain Drove and Rogue's Alley

To the rural dispossessed.
Fool raining down names, each one has its target
Ness, Gartree and Lafford
Alive to their new geography

Like snow at the wrong time of year
And Fool seen striding across fen dykes
Larger, more dangerous than before.

CHERRY PICKERS ON LEXICON ROAD

Their platforms are resting at crouched angles
Their pistons are lowered, heightened, lowered:
They have made an arrangement like panic
Climbing up the sky.

Then slowly one of them will awake
Edge forward with concentrated purpose
Shifting in sections
Like, as it were, a new arrival
Born from an overnight forging.

Above the corrugated sheds their skeletons rise:
Next to the pine trees they are kings
And the one-eyed container that serves as an office. Yes
Steadily one of them breaks free –

The wheels cracking harsh over thick gravel
The arched backs of its rivals
Clenched with restrained force.
They can't go anywhere yet, stuck in their capital letters
A lifetime locked in with their pistons
All things that hold them in place –

Until the minder arrives in a blue truck
And backs between them with care.

A TREASURY

And the red mud scrambles away into dust,
sunk pits cleaving tarmac onto the bone.

An army of stiff blades chops at the wind –
in turn it is trodden down

by an ancient need for certainty
in a place where nothing is fixed –

transitional light goes ranging
through clamped-down houses that seem

like toys on a destroyed board,
farms and their rusted tenders

signalling like ships
lost in a green bewilderness.

A glimmer of heat from the pasture
to say that all's burnt, finished, done.

Such colours shouldn't exist –
yellow scoring the retina –

they rip across the runways beyond Star Fen
windmilling troublesome joy,

the storybooks re-invented.
And when the roof is lifted off

you are flung up into it, thermals winding
you bright and transparent away,

striped gates bouncing up at the level crossing
saying if you are lucky, you can go.

THE ATTRACTIONS ARE CLOSED TODAY

It is always raining, it is raining again
It is piling down with pluvial generosity
As fast as the devil can spit –
There will never be any politeness about it
Because it is raining to hell and back
Where the houses crowd like unlovely teeth
And the acneous hillside, blistered with red estates,
Spreads its developing faultline.
This is indeed Mount Misery as marked on the map –
People are running with bags on their heads
To the dank shops' embrace;
Only the civic statues are brave enough
For this is a town of theatrical disillusion
Where under the sorrowful arms of streetlamps
A thousand hearts are slain.

CRANE OVER SWANPOOL

The god Arcomet
With Egyptian rigidity –
He covers almost the sky
Like a great stork.
Nobody is too distant as he wheels
In a protective circle.

The terrifying reach of the grabber
The chain, the prodding tines! No
We are not safe from his anarchic posturing
The inexorable slide-rule.
He'll have us in, down, out.

The shadow-finger points, moves, points…
Truly he bears an immense burden
A one-armed god
Inscribed on a brick monument.
Who patrols the highways
Carrying his son, the spider

In his netted cage.
Who denies all knowledge
Sweeping away the opposition.
Who conducts the wind oratorio
Saying 'Aaaaaaahhhhhh' –

THIS RIDE IS BOISTERIOUS

They are snatched away laughing
Their vulnerable legs hanging down.

They swing about briskly
Like popes in canisters,

Their pink runway is a blur –
Let me hear you scream

As the attraction whips on,
Strobe darts picketing the wreckage

And mixed lights shear the horizon,
News from our world

Maddened with plural fortune
Above the jumbled town;

The big wheel turns on its axis
Climbing with its cargo to the stars.

23 CONDITIONS OF SIGHT AND SILENCE

1. The tractor seriously ploughing with all ten fingers.

2. The wind turbines, exchanging their arms.

3. The trees, hung broken in sulphurous light.

4. Trees, with their skirts as far as the wheat.

5. Because you cannot tell where sky begins.

6. The kestrel over the marsh falls instantly.

7. The dogs loping down with steep heads.

8. The doves' voices, tumbling over each other.

9. The far farms, and their personal observance.

10. The weathervane knows where the wind lies.

11. And what kind of silence are you trying to hear?

12. The mist, developing in secret.

13. The hoofprints, pecking at the margins.

14. The chanterelles, floating through cracks in soft wood.

15. The birdlights weaving their counterpoint.

16. Your messages, lifted on wires.

17. The knotted clematis strangling the brickwork.

18. The building, wearing its patchwork coat.

19. The trees, now leaning asleep.

20. The white shirt illuminates the road.

21. The housefly, polishing its hands.

22. And what have you heard, or seen?

23. And what is the likelihood of loss?

BELVEDERE PARK

The children in descending order of size
Stare out across the terrace towards the sea.

The boys are dreaming of murderous deeds
As Father disappears behind *The Times*.

Soiled clouds beetle overhead.
Mother resumes her embroidery, stabbing away.

The bougainvillea blooms unnoticed.
The girls stick pins in their dolls, also unnoticed,

And Roger is lying down in a darkened room
Surrounded by medicine bottles, seven deep.

Peacocks echo on the distant lawn.
Dr. Benson is due to arrive just now

Bearing his latest device in a velvet-lined box
Which proved most effective at Malvern.

Ferns drift over the brick parterre
Their somnolent mist. Close blue settles around.

There will be a storm tonight, a wrecker
To set the weathervane spinning.

Across that verdure on patent feet
It is the butler Kensington who comes.

He takes a whole age to arrive
As the blue-eyed girls remain motionless.

Begging your pardon, Ma'am, he begins:
The private tutor is here, called Peter Quint.

MASTER OF WORKS

The parkland there, Sir
Not obtrusive to the casual eye

Its artifice concealed in the approved English manner.
Remark upon the left your small temple

– let us say, to Harmony or the Four Winds –
Advise me on the image immured within –

As if, Sir, the ancients themselves
Did pour their blessings on your fine estate.

You will find it an esteemed model
As seen in the later volumes of Vitruvius.

A humble façade, Sir,
Should not be countenanced here;

The correct gesture is worth an hundred lies.
I have designs, you may rest upon it –

When the population is cleared from the gate
You will have unbroken prospects.

BETRAYAL IN THE FORMAL GARDENS

Look at that, you say.
Are artichokes in season? I do not know.
By the topiary hedge
We should seem okay. Their finicking heads appear.
These pleasant vistas!

The long air of the afternoon
Slides down. I would rather not
Be here than there, not here, not there;
A dissociate possibility.
Such difficulty comes from not quite caring.

Between close-set hedges
An isolate pond appears. The lily flower
Sails out from the floating raft…
What need of you do I have?
Are you anything there to me? Was
There something I should have done, or said?
If I said this or that, what hooks do you have
To hold me to it?
I thought I wasn't real until I found you.

Where five lanes meet there are seven trees
An apple, and a rosebush. Choose
Yourself some thorns.
Hear the rooks cawing home.
R.I.P. says the tombstone, R.I.P.

LADDERS APPEAR AT FENCES

Brick sheds diminish, brambles lift over walls
gardens give onto wasteland, feet into miles

espalier trees link arms around the yard –
there is always stuff to be thrown out, junked, denied –

removals heap into skips, the engines growl
cucumbers fatten in cold-frames, greenhouses boil

gutter-pipes reach up at corners, bins wait in line
washing flies sidewards away from the wind,

sorrell burns the embankment, rust on the rail
the mainline goes elsewhere, channelled to change

and footballs barge into bushes, newspapers fall,
breadcrumbs are scattered on patios, curtains are drawn

children are playing at houses, adults too late
tenants touch up their paintwork, cars on display

lorries heave onto motorways, distances lead
flowerheads open their hands, and windows swing free

aerials jostle for signals, the programmes come
and every departure engenders a home,

carrots emerge from allotments, plugs pull on drains
ladders appear at fences, people climb.

SOMETHING HAPPENS, SOMETIMES HERE

From the open window plates clank into sinks.
Pampas grass, blue and sharp, thrusts a head.

Its rapiers wait, stiff with outrage
stuck in this dusty corner of rural Lincolnshire

home of lost causes and chimneypots.
A spindryer drones on down to a stuttering halt.

The River of Life Ministry proclaims God's kingdom
in faded handbills: *the wisdom of the wise is foolishness*

and: *Rottweiler puppy for sale, eight months old.*
A jet stripes its lonely line down the sky's big face.

It's Saturday, it's July, and nobody's out
the dance is cancelled, the caravans moved on

it's business as usual in silent towns
with window displays that haven't been changed

since the day the cinema was bombed in '44.
And junkyard houses march backwards

to green seas crested with kale, waterbutts, canes
the praiseworthy end of labours

and sheaves of Golden Rod. It's all in order, friends
your lives are pure there's nothing to reach you here

the kingdom is safe, the bunting flutters in peace
streaming from thick-legged architecture,

men will soon be home in their brylcreemed hair
your bakelite sets alive with plosive announcements…

I walk down a blind lane. Houses in curious brick,
tendrils escape from the sides of crumbling ledges

Grade 1 viola floats past. A piano goes stumbling after,
playlist to How I Began. And somebody comes.

BURROW MUMP, DEADENED BY THE SUN

Windows are open to let the badness out.
Hummocked cattle slump on the seething green.

The school bus arrives. It is packed full of chairs.
A taxi leaps over the bridge and disappears.

No no no says the butterfly's flight
Doddering over banked-up nettles –

Traffic lights scream *STOP* at the empty road,
Angles of buildings cut everyone's voices down.

BLOTOFT HALT

For then it was an imperial silence:
Two swans riding the skin off a ditch.

And I had missed the lone signal-
Man in his tall white tower
Cranking at levers like a man who starts up the world.

I thought a hare went fleering
Into the brown turbulence
Husks and furrows in one,
All set to wince off the planet:

And silos stilt the horizon like emissaries
From a place where nobody wakes.

This could be grass from Saturn
Present at the birth of flint –
Slow light cracking at the edge,
The witch-bushes fizzing in spite.

I am caught in a white-out
Whose only word is 'No'.

CANDLESHOE

The pollen was flying and the wind was out of its cage
I had negotiated a route of ancient cowpats

Even the lark could not go higher
Everything further away than I thought.

I heard crickets questioning in the grass
And dry yellow plants like struck matches

Gave me a hill of gold.
A mole had turned up the shining ear of a shell.

I was there on the earthstump looking at the grass
And a white feather travelled with me

As far as the fingerpost saying *Away*.
Behind me there were emptied barns

Proclaiming their innocent status,
The cows moved one to another

In their separate department.
Now I am head high in wild angelica and campion

Their scattered petals are beneath my feet.
Which one of you is my enemy?

Because I possess double fortune
Because I am Fool with my steeple hat

Creature of many directions
And my cathedral is limitless space.

I am she who embraces chaos –
My hand breaks through the spider's web

While sheep with their T-bar heads
Lie with the rook's feather undisturbed;

And when the sun walks over the rim
The standard thistle raises its violet lamp

Where Fool is, down in a roomful of grass.
I am there on the vacant manors

Rammed beneath the earth's parapet
Where tractors scale their lines –

Having no number I am everywhere
At the crossroads you'll see me vanish

At the point where needlebright damsel flies
Go practising their neon signs

And the insect shakes the bellflower
On the angled plains of Pelham's Land.

NO SIGN IN THE BURNING GLASS

A broad heath.
The sprayer chucks its arch, plume after plume.

A few late cabbage whites.
The bee has a look.

Corn rears up the slanting field
Tasselled cobs thick in the stem.

Ling has returned like a crooked finger
To the low wood brimming with flies.

Left cars grin at the verge.
Later, a nightjar trawls the air:

Sometimes you're looking for them,
A bird with scaly wings.

We think: Ah yes, the symbolic path
Ahead, it says, ahead,

No sign in the burning glass.

'and you shall see them face to face'

Here you can believe it.
Stone-riddled enclosures
The beck with its own language
And trees looking away.

She scrambled in her pinny
Straight from Chapel
The fist-sized stones kicking down
On what was termed later

A difficult climb.
Up, up into the spring blue
The wind streaming at her
Like the pure waters below,

And tufts of seeds sat
On the spears of sour rushes
The rust-hardened peat-hags
Panicked by sheep.

There were five men hanging
Like the crows and pests
Her Dad nailed up
To frighten the foxes,

Five men from the clouds
Their dead plane tumbled
Into the next valley
Like a lost tin lid.

The chapel bell teng-tenged
As voices raised
From Bield and Dale End
Hackett and Wilson's,

Work-sleeves rolled up
Under the stiff jackets,
Huge hands at rest
That could move the high fells

And lay braided pines
Tender and careful
To the chopping mills,
And free the snagged sheep

From the tearing barbs.
The men were brought down
From the sharpened rock
And cruel shades,

Arranged like heroes
As if they had lived
On the same earth as these.
Reluctant leavers

They broadcasted thanks
On the ghostly wires,
Vanished in lanes
To labourers, not dreamers,

Faces, images
Parade-ground perfect
Flashed out, lenticular
Approaching them; gone.

WAPENTAKE

Overnight the landscape had submitted.
Where fields were, it was flood
Black pans lipping at the rim.
And where the trees were, there was the wreck
Of drowned men, stark arms
Come back to warn us too late.
At the dike side there was wet sedge
Seeming to throw its pale hair down
And the perfect heron was not there:
The tumult of ice had thrown him
Far beyond the year's wheel.
And the town I was near had foundered
Like a tilting barque,
The screech of steel cable and wire
Dragging it back to the head.

THE PLAQUE, THE CHANDELIER, THE BOX OF TRICKS

They are setting out chairs for an event
Shaking the wretched animals apart with both hands

But the fatal flower arrangement is about to fall
And the troublesome microphone leans

In a stunned way, swinging its head
Like a mad cow selected for slaughter.

Any minute now the audience will arrive
After the furniture has staged the event.

The chairs will be smug with their backs to the wall
They know about chaos theory.

Soon he will arrive, the Event Devil
Claiming that he is in charge from now on

Him and his multiple hat disorder.
Already the performers do not occur –

People are walking backwards from the room
Until the air is sucked out finally,

Only the paper elephant survives,
The plaque, the chandelier, the box of tricks.

ALBA: Normal Service Will Be Resumed

Dearest, awake, the night has fled
        the milk van rattles along the street
it's time the sheets were off, get up
        the moon has put her eye out. Come,

swains and others are stumbling over their shoes
        cannot find their shirts, their office bag. Arise
it is time accounts were settled and files were out
        children launch themselves at common school
and teachers all must find the heart to move.

Look at the Ford Mondeos streaming away
        kettles prickle to life across the town
postmen clack the letterbox flaps
        delivering joy. O love you must depart

for Phoebus rises to the power of ten,
        yappity wives and deadbeat husbands alike
must greet the day like victims dragged anew.
        Do not burrow beneath the duvet, love,
because it is eight, the chariot lumbers on

and much remains to be accomplished. Go,
        lovers must always part, and there is the door
normal service will be resumed,
        the stars have fallen out of sight.

LOSE THE LUMBERING SPACECRAFT OF OUR LIVES

The message you never posted is probably there
hiding under the piles of built-up regrets:

the interviewer you might have met, the stormy love
his hopeless wreckage under a second-class stamp,

the saddest things, those undelivered cards
the wishes of nations shuddering into sacks

and bothersome minor relations you won't come across
unless it's by shock, at parties you always hate

the letters you want to blitz right out of your time
falling like itchy confetti, a snowfall of blight

belonging to different towns, the addresses on wrong
or were they never collected, or really gone

or should we make as much effort as we have
to lose the lumbering spacecraft of our lives?

HART'S GROUNDS

Pink bindweed is forcing its way through the wall,
red ants trickle in a line
and I'm no nearer to you than I was.

The full heads of corn have been swept away,
so many people
where had they come from,
a churchyard crammed with the living.

Their laughter rings across the fields
as the combine harvester grazes,

people, swatting at flies and carrying trays.
They waver out of the hall
like bees at a hive,
their young dogs weave around the trestles.

You know the instant when the light
                        has shifted its meaning
you do not know how the summer ends,
the parties glanced at through branches

their cakes, their sticky ledges.

And where were you in this scene,
returning an hour later
no sight of the dancers at all –

the combine harvester fresh from new plunder
cramping itself down the lane,

green and red, red and green.

FOOL ENSURES THE GUIDEPOSTS ARE STRIPED
BLACK AND WHITE

Sheltering trees are rushing their branches across –
here it is never still, you could swear
the roads had twitched their skeins overnight,
a new passage opens, departs.

In a meadow between two bridges
Fool pegs out a brand new demesne.
This one, O this one, Fool
will have free entry. No appointments are needed.

A hoverfly with its helmet of eyes
inspects and settles for a while.
Tok! Tok! go the fenceposts, deep underground
connecting descended heights, one to another.

Approach with silence and reverence:
the rowan with its hands full of berries
the harvestman bowling in its wheel of legs.
The sky blows hot and cold in its work for existence.

There is rubble, stuck through the hill's motley coat
And dry-wired plants
the matchwood houses can't outlast –
loose doors are ripped from their hinges overnight.

And Fool is climbing the limestone terrace
more long rails than you'd ever imagine
bristling from her back. They're going in,
nailing the shifted pastures
to their last known positions.

SANCTUARY

I have to go there, have to
It's not a question of when.
Of course, it can stand in for anywhere you like
The names are not specific.
It's not always pretty
The houses won't increase their value year on year
It's not that kind of place.

There's no photographs can do it justice
They come out blank, or wrong.
It's hard to find –
No maps seem to go there
It's swerved by every road.
You grow chilled, wary, lost,
It's always over that next hill
You ask and ask but there's no answer.

'in darkness let me dwell'

My real life is out there and somebody's got it.
They caught it through my slippery fingers, they're steaming

Headway up the coastal route on the outside lane
Making for an enlarged future. I've been spat out

Like a flawed diamond –   even the photographs are rare,
A lunatic judge swings me up by the heels braying

Back to your cage, little pointless one
These people have important things to do

What makes you think it is possible after all?
Believe me, this is a serious time to be worried –

A zany drives your wheels. It is
The vicious laughter of empty masks and circuses:

Their blowsy music rasps on… there won't be an audience
As they glare you down to the pit.

A dark complex has foundered me,
Clamped down and airless, the clutch of well-shafts and water.

THE JUBILEE BRIDGES

Great river forgive me
I am not one of your children
still you converge on a mystical north
like all four fingers on the same hand.
And now I know why people return:
the stacked bridges one above another
your seven-decked centripetal city
shelving up from your resting arm.
But you are not my city even though
you have me in your pocket
your bridges busy with deep communication
crosscut with flying banners
of the world's unresting transport
arrowed straight at your heart,
for a second each one suspended
then moving in perfect concord
scaling like threaded-on beads
in the illusion we're all free.
And look, your city is wearing its jewelled band
its levels gone stripy with roads
your arches are raising their eyebrows
from the river's silted bed,
your girders resting lightly
on hidden foundations,
climbing with pluralist buildings
a bridge in time for leaping across
the space, a bridge for everything
every bridge in its place.

TALISMAN

I am Fool, wind-hammered
collecting my bag of trash.
Always, always I say
the dappled grass is not enough
to call you home.

There was chequered light moving the walls
and without warning a leveret clattered down
straight into my place, pulsating –
a brown earth star, too terrified to move.

He imagined he was invisible.
Fool and the meaning of Hare –
you are left to your own conclusions
famed for speed.

Here, Fool, is your talisman
struck from a crack in the green: one
who thinks it is not there. It fell out
like a creature pushed
from a slung purse in the air.

Fool, out on the wires –
you do not know it is the storm
that shelters you, that the widest spaces
produce the least harm.
What are you doing here,
in the loose community of four winds
walking through barns you don't own?

And fresh light blinks through planks, makes stars
gates still slamming on gateposts, barely contained

farmdogs springing like green twigs
bent and let go.

        Later, there is more –
a broken ceramic ornament
from the lost god of telegraph poles
who otherwise marches on, his messages
crackling like fire in his hair.

A MASQUE FOR DANCING

> Antigua
> engraved and improved
> a rock, even with the water
> a house spider works its way up the wall
> a scale of English miles,
> gold flecks on Murano glass.

> Running late
> quarter of an hour
> electric points under tabbed boards
> children with their heads under the curtain
> stuffed heads
> Rules of the Eton Society
> "This Is The Looking Table"
> hats hung on antlers
> stains on the wallpaper
> stains on the boards,
> the Wreck of Sir Cloudesley Shovell in *The Association*.

> Pink blossom drifts on the gravel path:
> in two small garden marquees
> the children begin their sandwiches
> more dropped twigs from the tree
> a safe with 11 ingenious locks
> worked by the same fork.
> Sir Francis in red
> Anne of Bohemia
> Mary Queen of Scots, a jewel
> at her prized throat.
> In every room there's a unicorn,
> we must look for the fabled beast.

THE PILGRIM APPROACHING FROM A DIFFERENT ROAD

Just as mine host was talking about the lightning-strike
a tractor waddled into view.
It was my 50th visit to heaven
still finding the whole place different.
Today the lines are more marked on the field itself
as though recent rain had defined them.

Five grey birds are turning like knives
in sudden unseasonal wind.

> It is Sunday –

only the farmers are out,
wobbling in their warm high cabs.
They are finding reasons to go somewhere,
farmers and the tearoom patron.
He carries his weight like a careful package.

'The bricks were raining down everywhere in the village,
plugs blown out of their sockets…'
The crusty groundwarp itself a cause of activity:
elbows ready to rise.

And I have six more miles before the clouds race in before the rain,
past the hieratic sugarbeet factory
in its armoury of brick and steel,
past the hardboiled smallholdings
clamped to the river's straight edge.

A chiffchaff is sharpening its whetstone.

'Disintergrated,' the man said.
Where the thunderbolt struck it shattered
a metre of solid masonry and its concrete bed.

NEW PLANTATION

They are the small fizzing planets we must not lose the sight of.
Each one has an eccentric orbit.

When one of them swings out beyond the rest
He's the one you must catch up first.

We are pushing them in through that gate over there
We don't care how long it takes

Of course there's always one who won't go in –
We select the biggest lever, lean on

Crank him towards the exit.
The ones in front are pulling

They won't let go, not now
You push hard, then harder

The planets will line up somewhere at some point in the future
We'll be there.

THE REMOVAL OF STONE HOUSE

Brick by brick the old
asylum tumbles,
the tower of Elysium falls:
leaves blown away.

In maze after maze
the terrified people go round –
extraordinary voices call,
each one losing sight
of their other selves.

We are here, there, and beyond it:
split to a thousand atoms
those numerous voices!
The spray of a firework
completely undefended.

Animals howl like a night
stuck with souls.

'took my sign to the crossroads'

At the crossroads she looked both ways.
Only the reedmace and its padded truncheon
Stuck from the stagnant tributary
Of a plate-metal river.

And her rucksack shifted
From shoulder to shoulder
In rising heat. Certainly it felt like a storm's weight
Pressing its body close.

A faint tremor beneath her
An uncertainty –   a dust-cloud –
She doesn't know what happened –
In an instant the Master appeared

Like a zip-flash comic rocket.
He clumped forward on his trademark hooves.
I've been waiting for you,' he said,
'Now what can I give you in return

For your not so precious soul?'
The brimstone eyes drilled closer.
'Well?' croaked the Master
Smoke issuing from his nostrils

Curled horns ridged and polished
Like a prize Derbyshire ram.
There was bone at his overshot brow
At his ironshod farmyard feet.

Fool in the red-soaked darkness
The earth falling away,
Fool pinched beween thumb and forefinger
Grey nails grubby with gravemould.

Held there caught in the calipers
Every second smaller and smaller
Like a speck in a whale's eye –
Inspected, turning in a circle

And the common toadflax threw its torches
Star-braided eyebright and bog myrtle
Far off in the receding pastures,
A postcard lifting in space

Like a flake off a shelled egg.
Fool face down in a rustbucket
Somewhere beyond the bypass,
Sour milk dribbled in the gutter

The whap of thundering lorries
Aiming their loads across,
The hiss of slick tyres on tarmac,
Wet cardboard and rubble cement.

The hot rank goat-stink
Thick about her head: *where am I?*
Fool had embarked on an old journey
She didn't know it yet.

THE DOUBLE MEANING OF AERIALS

The aerials are perched like flightless birds
They open their skeletons to the sky
Their displayed angles are tang and attitude.

Of all pernickety tangles in life's blue
You are the most linear
Which I like utterly,
Broadcasting your ballet on the rooftops
In your language from Neptune.

And that one there has the aspect of a short farmer
                                        carrying a rake
And this one lances towards the West
                                        in a thicket of nails.

You could hang your washing on their dread scopes
Count the raised fishbones and
The plated-on satellites of chance
Cluttering in the same way
Like a jungle of coathangers
In the universe cupboard.

They are the avid fascinators
                        on our patient houses,
They are the caricatures –

I am going to climb up there and do strange music
Rattle a stick across their railings
Play scarecrow sounds on their nerves.

SUNDAY IN THE PARK AT THE END OF THE WORLD

> *Destiny, give it back to Bolan.*
> *Now.*
> *Now, please....*

and the yew hedge is trimmed to the shapes of melted plastic
somebody's project gone wrong

cones upside down and helter-skelters

NO BALL GAMES NO CYCLING
through the gate and turn left
We Are An Outdoor Cafe
Three Phase Socket Below

and whatever we do we cannot get the acoustics right
the front-man waves like an umpire
black stands scissor apart
the banner goes up:

nothing on this channel, Dave, he shouts
as people walk under the hedges
with multiple legs.

The audience re-arranges itself
like a selection of burst balloons
we aim our plank of noise at the furthest bench

– it is the Wall Of Sound –

sing Happy Birthday, Mary our front-man instructs
as a child on a metal scooter screeches past
one of its castors jammed

and the molten hedges are crowding in
the larches dangle their hands
we are condemned
two hours of tame thrashing
at an outdated repertoire –   run
my friends, run

and somewhere a fountain is switched on
their name liveth for evermore....

                    Say sorry! the mother screams
                  pointing from one child to another

THE NEWBOROUGH COUNTY BYPASS ENQUIRY
ACHIEVES CONFUSION

The morality of not paying for a road!
(laughter in the hall)

Already three to two against (sorry) *in favour* of our route –
they won't stand up and say it's wrong
(graphic demonstration)

Mr. Inspector!
This statement is the same as the *last* one
presented to the Public Enquiry:

His proposal for a road is TOTALLY IMPRACTICAL
it's all that's left of an ancient wood
often been fought for, e.g.

water authority knocking trees down
gravel pit/brickworks/motorway/old airstrip
motorcyclists' racing track…

And we know of three landowners who would not object
to what is known as the Objectors' Route.

If others can give their reasons
so can I (said the man waving a paper
who unfortunately could not be heard)

There are probably many alternatives
we are dropping behind timetable, gentlemen

We had professional advice and paid the man his money!
(antagonistic, with his flapping pen)

Well it *still* goes across my land
but in a DIFFERENT DIRECTION.

I only know how, as an ordinary person
not used to technicalities, one with a mortgage…

THE NEIGHBOURHOOD SOCIAL WORKER EXHIBITS SOME SIGNS OF FATIGUE

you can't believe what anyone says these days
I mean they have hundreds stashed away
and they always say they've got nowt
this woman, she started to have hysterics
you do what you can they never appreciate it
they ask for money all the time
and when you can't get it they have hysterics
we can only work according to the book
and they always think you can get them more money
all the time, it's what they ask for…

Well I was really put on the spot –
the department told me down the phone
look in her cupboards they said
and see if she's got any food in
because she said she had nowt at first
that was when she started having hysterics
never been told to look in people's cupboards
that's a new one on me that is
but they tell you anything these people
and you can't trust any of them.

THE SILENT WITNESS

The trees mean something tonight
I hear them rushing the border
Over the dark road –
Threshing an upswept crown,
Their thick arms denying.

You could forget where you are,
How many times travelled
On that same road –
The guilt, the incredible waiting,
A silent witness
At the corner of my eye

And the road narrows,
Twisting further inside –
A silence without knowing,
The grey ghost waiting
And the fear of staying, of going.

CERULEAN CHINA EYES

warmhearted..... *real*
        yes
unearthed,   and   (gently)   fabulous
a   perfect   *gem*   that
unspoiled   rural
      community, y'know?   dear
little, and so......   with its rare
             crochet tabs and
             willow bats, jam
             the Famous
             Five and their floppy lashings
             of ginger beer dog
– can't you imagine it
Ferdinand,   they   even
have   yellow   sand
         Oh
my genuine
gosh
there's a vintage charabanc jolting across our sightlines
with ladies in Sunday hats

                  so turn on your video capture
                  my braves! and
                  get those week-
                  end des. res
                  supplement pics, they'll want
                  to live here forever, you deep
                  organic dinkiest cup-
                  cake mother of the
                  cushioned shires. How
                  they yearn for You
                  your biscuits and bees, your true
                  cerulean china eyes,
                  in the tough trough
                  of caverned cityville!

                    Yes
we'll spearhead this,
this natural revolution, comrades –
snap up that good green
funding *now*
                    you're only
1 deprived borough away, listed
source of nu-wave bit-part
jobs:
                    Noddy and
                    Big Earz
                    Welcumz U
                    the arty crafty teatime
                    of the new republic,

            comb-over grassland 1 bulb short
            awful afeard o' strangers
            mister
            specially ones in
            big hats
            bells
            bladders

......told us the *best* spots   cheese
            locals,   and   quaint
            must-have
                    striped   awnings   yes
            cranberry   features
                            windowsills
                    real mould
            grown in the Coronation Hall
                            authentic

            artisan *boules* to die for

WE MOVE THROUGH YOUR DISTRICT AS AVATARS

Comrades, we have spray-painted your sheep.
We have re-arranged your signposts. We
have knitted you a circus.

We have erected high bronze sculptures of naked men;
we have strutted, carrying drums.
You say you are not happy.

We have given you the sound-garden
of a Cold War early warning system.
We have cut up books and burnt them and thrown them.
We have held a Potato Festival

and a Sausage Festival.
Still you are not happy.

We have trained you in the creation of abstract mosaics.
Sent our ambassadors among you
bearing beads and shells.

Yes, our storytellers drag rainbows behind them.
Our dancers describe the infinite zodiac
using only the medium of their two hands.

We have come to your remote settlements
as dolphins before the wave.
We are your friends,
we come in peace.

Next year there will be a Sausage *and* Potato Festival.
You say you are not happy.

Next we will send you the Red Skeleton of Death,
our two articulated golden birds.

THE BRICK OF EVERYONE GETS IN MY WAY

This is a blues song baby.
Lincolnshire is like that, with its repeat pattern.
I mean –   it is a *song*
one where the heart is open
though everything else is as bad as it was before.

Our separate state rides out like a loamy island
in four-dimensional blues –
you'll know it's not like anywhere else you've seen
the way our fields are pegged out for inspection.

The stilt-horses of a Dali painting
are lining across the rim.
The yellow plains are the same here
as in distant Figueres, or the madness of Cervantes.

They are shaking you upside down
in the jungle-box of images –
so let's declare independence
from whatever the poets would have us believe.

And when the brick of everyone gets in my way
and nobody knows what trouble you've seen
remember this landscape as a song –
one with a freefalling cadence,

your rusting trailers and picket fences
beneath astonishing blues,
your four-armed cast-iron signpost
deciding the middle of nowhere.

ALL THAT NOW REMAINS

This road is out on a limb.
Epiphany, and the kings are finally there.
Plates of colour are flung at my head
Another state of absolutes.

I will never see it entirely –
The raft is too unstable.
One by one the stones will venture up
Like the fabled drowned city.

They are buried and reburied.
GRIMERS says the trailer, parked aside.

Everything now has changed –
The full-headed hawthorns have lost their hair
Rooks bank up in the west
The regular cattle are barned away.
Rabbits are digging their own cathedral.

It was not now the graveyard of kings.
Only the bonerack hogweed bristling out
This is their army crumpled about the stones.

A grey horse is looking at me, the only thing moving.
The noise I am hearing is the sound of my own coat.

The clumps have struck out their sparks
Only the fenceposts are holding this land together
The gate is left open
Everything else has fled,

A tree lies frozen in mid-stretch
The barbs in its hands still lively.
A slow water crawling
That wasn't here before

And I am sure this place is a ring
I have stumbled along the causeway into it
Like Fool in the seven nets.

THE SPLINTERS

You have let them down
the greenhouses capsized,
tables on their knees.
You cannot save them, not now
their looped polythene trailing
like rainforest lianas
light piercing the grey fleece.

Their soft curtains are falling
into history's long chest
but the plants keep on growing
yellow, gargantuan, spined
under the loft layers
backs pressed hard at the corners
fists hitting and hitting
until they blind the glass.

We are coming, they say
we are through the shattered mile
our branches are out
we are carrying our frames.

THE RAKES

Crossing the burning plain I come
to the power station's upturned bed.

This is where old energy comes to die,
a barge setting out through slow washes.

We are somewhere east of the Grand Cut
in a place without visible sides. I am walking with Fool

who is mounting a big disappearance.
And the windmills are bowling for their lives

in subtle gradations. As I swing past
their cyclic triads, I find an outrider

a short one waving frantically
like the guest at an elegant party

who simply can't make himself heard –
it must have the work of ten

billowing through the atmosphere like that.
For all his effort he will never catch up

it's the wrong side of the tracks
he's the unexpected joker in the deck.

Their tips travel the horizon: *come this way*
where we are not seen flying our wings

there are three-dimensional clouds over here
like giant stage-sets moving themselves.

IS

Admit honesty:
truth is
changing me up

let me speak
you, for I
am both monster
and creator,

a Caliban
who became Ariel

you are my speech
my language,
not one thing made

the land using me
for its own ends

not yet
thought of

I want to know
the world exten-
ded a kind finger,

it is
it is
praise
it is

like this